TALES OF A MODERN DAY AESOP

Tasos Yacalis

This book is dedicated to the dream that all our efforts to attain knowledge and achieve wisdom will someday lead to understanding.

PROLOGUE

When I think of the loss of Robin Williams (along with many other fine human beings) who could easily be classified as the most gifted comedian of our times, I ask myself, "Where did we miss? Why couldn't we reach, understand his deeply hidden pain or help him overcome it?"

Our approach or ways we try to help others need modification. We need to be far more flexible. To feel "alive" every human being needs to have a sense of self-worth and personal dignity. This is what is essential to their wellbeing and happiness. It means at times we have to enter their world and fight the necessary battles alongside them. Confining ourselves to office or house visits with artificial time schedules does not work for everyone. Life is just not that way.

The following true stories are some of my humble efforts to achieve this.

A MODERN-DAY WITCH HUNT

Sevi was born on one of the beautiful Greek islands in the Ionian Sea. It was an environmental paradise but rarely experienced in this way since she lived and grew up in the worst of impoverished conditions. She and her entire family were shunned by their neighbors who saw them as the "scum" of the neighborhood.

Her mother's behavior was most often out of the bounds of reality. She fluctuated in her thoughts and actions with irreverent instability. A fanatical Christian, she continuously filled Sevi's growing years with frightening stories of supernatural happenings. She would formidably accentuate how the devil and saints were always present to punish anyone who deviated from their religion's prescribed code of conduct.

Rejected by almost everyone, Sevi would accept any kind of work, no matter how impossible the conditions or pay. Only jobs no one else wanted to do were offered to her. Devoid of stable guidance or controls, her vision of life and the world were dominated by fear. Her behavior often simulated that of a feral child who had just stepped out of the jungle. She would sneak into people's houses when the occupants were away steal food from the kitchen, devour it with a crude voraciousness, stuffing it into her mouth with her bare hands.

By the age of eighteen she had blossomed into a beautiful young woman who never went by unnoticed by the men in the village. One such man, Antonis, took a closer look. He was a crude but successful businessman who was among the wealthiest on the island. He pursued Sevi and finally convinced her to marry him. She became pregnant almost immediately and had a son about a year later.

Understandably her devastating childhood had made her very insecure and desperate in her search for love. Her selection of a soul mate was a disaster. Antonis was an alcoholic, abusive, sadistic and viciously cruel in his attitudes and actions. Once, during her pregnancy, he kicked her in the groin while screaming at her that she was "a worthless piece of shit" and she should go back to her crazy mother.

Abuse and rejection were commonplace for Sevi, she had experienced it all of her life. With all of the negatives there was one powerful positive, she had learned to adjust. A deeply buried hate and hostility had made her "tough", at least on the surface. One day, while Antonis was at work, she stole the money he kept hidden in the house, packed whatever of her things she could carry in her suitcase, wrapped her one year old baby in a sling around her body and left. She arranged to sail on a boat heading for the mainland and settled in a small town. Without ever contacting Antonis again she managed to divorce him.

The tragedy of her life's circumstances had left her with a lifelong, irreversible dilemma. she was like two different people housed in one. The hate and desire to hurt others remained bitterly inside her but was countered by her guilt and fear of eternal damnation.

Panic would overwhelm her whenever she recalled her mother's stories about Michael, the arch angel, the punisher of evil doers and extractor of human souls. She had an icon of him in her room. It was surrounded by lighted candles which she fearfully never allowed to burn out. There were also crosses, beads and a pair of shoes nearby. This because in her hometown village many people swore they had actually seen the angry Archangel walking around in shoes. Paradoxically religion was the foundation of her serenity. In her new home, she changed her religion to an even more fanatical one. A change she felt was essential to her future welfare.

Sevi was not just a beautiful woman, she was born with a "piercing" intellect and blessed with a "gift of gab". These became invaluable talents when she opened a small business. The business' immediate growth was founded upon it. She made it a point to get to know and visit every beauty parlor in her town. It was like finding buried treasures in the middle of nowhere.

Using the powerful, ubiquitous components of gossip she became a very convincing saleswoman. Every one of her "high quality" products was deliciously supplemented with a very tasty morsel of the latest scandal.

She used her anger to disrupt her competition. It was uncanny to observe the ease with which she could get her competitors arguing with each other then slyly walk away from the discussion.

Her financial security did not come only from her

business. She was acutely aware of the ease with which she could attract men sexually and eventually manipulate them into giving her money and gifts.

Strict and consistent attendance to her church group helped to offset her guilt over her errant thoughts and actions. Her religious adherence continued to remain as the bed rock of her emotional stability.

Whether it was hormones or just the beauty of the day, Sevi innocently confessed to the leader of the group that she often had sexual fantasies about men. His immediate response was that she had committed the deadliest of sins. Reprimanding her, he angrily demanded that she must now appear before the group's religious court to be judged.

We all have some understanding of what fear is. We have all experienced it in varying degrees in our lives but it is almost unimaginable to feel what Sevi felt at that moment. She lived in a state of inconceivable panic until the day of the trial.

Appearing before this "symbolically God created divine panel of judges", she was commanded to respond to their demands. "Admit that you are possessed by the devil or you will be excommunicated". Panic stricken, trembling uncontrollably, in an almost inaudible voice, she courageously replied, "I am not possessed by the devil". She was immediately excommunicated by the screaming, hysterical panel. She was labeled a "contaminated persona non-grata" who was destined to burn in the fires of hell.

Overwhelmed by fear, guilt and an almost uncontrollable rage which she could not take out on the initiators, she succumbed to depression. What frightened her even more was that she was unable to sleep as suicidal fantasies began to dominate her thinking. It was why and how we first met. Truthfulness was never her greatest asset so under the guise of trying to help someone who was desperately in need of help but unable to ask for it, she asked if I could drop by her store to discuss the matter. She was so persuasive and challenging in the way she presented the situation, I decided to go along with her manipulation. Besides, I had always found it more rewarding and productive when you reach out and work with others in their own setting.

We worked together for many years with all the stresses, ups and downs present in every therapeutic relationship. Everyone needs their own time to find themselves. Sevi showed the beginning of the end was near when I visited and she had laid out on the floor, the icon of the avenging angel, his shoes and all of the religious paraphernalia she had collected through the years.

I vividly remember to this day the happy smile she had on her face when she said to me, "I want you to have the privilege of throwing all this junk in the garbage". My response, "No Sevi, this is an honor you must bestow upon yourself".

End of story? No. Some years later Sevi telephoned me. With a distinct feeling of satisfaction, she said, "you know what happened today?" I answered, "no, what?" "The leader of the group that excommunicated me paid me a visit. He said he wanted to talk to me, so I let him in. We walked into the living room. I sat on the sofa and he on an arm chair opposite me. Very shortly into the conversation he impulsively stood up, came over to where I was and sat next to me. He told me that I was a very beautiful woman and that he was always attracted to me. At that point he took me in his arms and tried to kiss me."

I leave it to the reader's imagination to visualize what happened next. I will simply say that Sevi was not only beautiful and intelligent but very strong and courageous and hell hath no fury like a woman excommunicated.

Moral

The devil was a remarkably ingenious creation of man to absolve him of personal responsibility for all of his devious thoughts and actions.

THE PLANET PANUTOPIA

Problems and pressures are ever present in our lives. We move with the tide, go with the flow and ride with the waves to survive. When we have the strength and flexibility within us we make it. When we can't we look for outside supports. If that fails we withdraw or break down. That's what happened to Alan who was the head of research in one of the largest hospitals in New York. He was likeable, friendly, highly respected by everyone and considered to be a genius. In the ten years he had worked in the research center he had gone into areas of medical research previously uncharted. His discoveries had led to significant changes not just for the hospital but for the medical profession in general. He was looked upon as the source of great expectations, the more he did the more was expected of him. Unable to withstand the mounting pressures he cracked and retreated into silence.

For weeks he would sit staring into space while I attempted to communicate with him. One day, as if he had just arrived, he looked straight at me and said, "I have just returned from my planet Panutopia. They have elected me President, I'm in the process of selecting my cabinet and I've decided to make you Minister of Future Organization and Change". I tried to hold back my pleasant but somewhat conflicted surprise and just smiled. Recovering, I thanked him for his faith in me. What a magnificent happening! In one simple statement he had opened the door to recovery.

I could now enter into his world, understand his pain and at least try to reconstruct a fine human being who was a struggling intellectual giant.

He had reversed our roles. Alan was now the leader, guiding me over strange, unusual and unknown paths, a potentially perilous journey for a psychotherapist. The pressure was now on me. What a clever maneuver, the unique power of the unconscious!

In the following days he smothered me with assignments. "The planet Earth is diseased", he emphasized, "is full of madness, hate and destruction. You must come up with a plan to place it in quarantine, to be forever isolated from any contact or communication with any other body in space. I expect a plan to be on my desk by tomorrow".

By placing a ridiculous time factor on something so important, which, logically would require considerable thought and preparation, he was unconsciously but cleverly revealing the stupidity and insensitivity of the request. He was also expressing, again in a hidden way, the anger that had accumulated within him for being placed in that position for who knows how many times. The research projects were always privately funded, hence the time limitations placed upon them.

Once we had the Earth out of the way we went on to organize everything on Panutopia. There were to be no armies, no separate nations, no religions, none of the usual philosophies or political systems that divided the oneness of humanity. There would be no police since every family would grow up in harmony, with love. To steal or hurt anyone would be unthinkable. Love thy neighbor and do unto others as you would have others do unto you would become the ubiquitous law of the land.

"What about money and financing?" I asked. Alan confidently replied, "There wouldn't be any. No need for money to exist at all." There he really put it to me. "I need you to form a society without the need of money". "Wow", I said to myself, "How in the world am I going to come up with an answer within a week?", because that was all the time he gave me. Stressing once more the ignorance with which we use our invented concept of time.

My hastily contemplated suggestion was that every family living on the planet would have its own home and small plot of land, enough to grow its own food and vegetables. Everyone would contribute their individual talents for building each other's houses. Whatever food was unavailable would be obtained by trading one talent for another.

Those who would not be interested or challenged by farming could study the remedies of nature for different diseases. Others could become technicians, inventors, entertainers, plumbers, carpenters or whatever they chose to be.

Everyone would take turns in suggesting and arranging the best way to organize things. Power would never be centralized in any individual or group. Of course he demanded all of this in specific written detail.

"What about health and education?", that was the

next barrage. "Closed rooms or buildings are not essential to learning", I replied. We could do it as the ancients did, asking questions of and learning from one another. We would begin by teaching how to be good human beings before learning how to read and write, how to be sensitive to one another's needs. Establish ethical principles and goals. Truth towards oneself and others is essential to psychological and somatic wellbeing and is one with love and happiness. Everyone has creative abilities within them. Only truth and harmony within the self allows them to emerge." As we progressed I could sense a softening in Alan. His demands were not as dictatorial or authoritative as they were at the start. "Who is going to govern and how?", were his next questions. I answered with a practical life example. "When a child feels loved and you grant him a sense of dignity, he will establish his own controls naturally. You don't have to tell a loved child what or how to do it. This holds true for adult human beings as well. Love brings out the best in all of us. Laws are made for people who disobey them. A kind, caring world would run itself. To frighten and control are the weapons of egotists whose only motive is to service their own selfish needs and desires."

Just as how he surprised me the first time he began to speak, he came in one day, looked at me with the most compassionate of expressions and said, "Hey doc, you don't really believe all these things could ever be, do you?" I knew then that Alan had come back to us.

Moral

Love is the greatest teacher. It enlivens, enriches and generates the strength to express the creativity that is within as all.

The creation of a theoretical God to show as how to think and act would be unnecessary, if we have faith and trust in one another. That trust would naturally direct our behavior. In essence what God would have realistically asked of us if he did in fact exist. Wherever love is we see our theoretical God come alive.

IN SEARCH OF HAPPINESS

Happy people never want to die. I suppose it is why we have created so many ingenious theories and philosophies about life after death. Still no one has ever returned to tell us what it is all about. Wouldn't it be wonderful if we knew with certainty we would never be separated from those we love, that somehow, somewhere we would find each other and live unto infinity. But we have no genuine evidence for that so we strive in this one life we are sure about to do the best we can.

If there is one thing I have learned in all the years I have been working with human beings, it is, life without love, is meaningless. The tragedy is, in our efforts to find it we often lose our way, so we experiment with additives. Things outside of ourselves, like drugs and cultish practices to do what we should accomplish from within. Alcohol is one of the most destructive of those additives.

James was a colleague. In Greece, the government assigns young doctors to small towns and villages to be sure there is a medical presence everywhere. This usually lasts for a year, they then move on to their selected specialty. Generally, they service minor medical problems, their basic task is to write prescriptions. It is how we first met, I needed a prescription so I went to see him.

Over time we had many pleasant conversations, in the process getting to know each other. He showed from the start he would make a fine doctor. He was kind, considerate and caring. What was also evident, his hands had a slight tremor and he tended to be "jittery" in his speech and movements, so it was no surprise when he said, "I'm planning to become a neurologist". Many years later James returned to our island and opened a practice as a neuro-psychiatrist. In an effort to help him get started I referred as many clients as I could to him.

His private practice did not go well so he accepted the position of the psychiatrist in the local public hospital. I understood why when I went to visit him there one day.

Outside of his office, in the hallway, were standing two police officers. They were anxiously pacing back and forth. I asked them, "You look worried, what's wrong?" They simultaneously replied, "Go inside and you'll see". I knocked, James told me to enter and I did.

Legal procedure dictates in Greece when someone is brought up on charges of drug abuse, he must undergo a psychiatric examination. The police had brought the detainee to his office for that reason but James was dead drunk. I suggested to him that we could perhaps salvage the situation if he allowed me to complete the testing for him and he agreed. I went outside and informed the policemen and they relaxed. Reentering I sat down at the desk and continued the examination. James was standing alongside me muttering something under his breath. With a sudden impulsive sweep of his hand he knocked everything off the desk and started yelling, "Those bastards Batsos", an epithet similar to the term "pigs" used in America. I sat him down, escorted the prisoner back to the police and told them that the examination could not possibly be conducted that day and must be rescheduled.

I spoke to James afterwards emphasizing he needed help and if he was accepting of me I could work with him therapeutically. It took time but he reluctantly agreed. James did not believe in psychotherapy. His belief was psychotropic drugs were the answer for all psychological problems.

To believe someone who is alcoholic would be able to keep scheduled appointments with consistency would be foolish. You have to reach out to them, so I visited him in his home. Most usually he would be in bed already under the influence of alcohol. Later, when he knew I was coming he would not drink but as soon as I left he headed straight for a liquor store. This went on for several weeks until we both admitted we weren't getting anywhere. I told him he was totally incapable of placing limits upon himself and the only solution would be to voluntarily sign himself into a clinic that specialized in the treatment of alcoholism. I offered, "I will return tomorrow morning and we will spend the entire day together discussing it". He accepted the suggestion.

When I arrived the next day he was already a little "tipsy". You may judge my next move to have been foolish and dangerous and you would probably be right but I had to show him I had faith and believed in him so I let him drive. There were two choices of how to reach our destination, a beach front restaurant on the other side of the island. By flat straight roads which was the longer way or a shortcut over the mountain. He chose the latter.

I cannot say I was relaxed but I tried to be. My hands were in the position and poised to grab the steering wheel with, I believe something close to the speed of light but it never became necessary. In a couple of hours he was completely sober and we sat conversing all the while until nightfall. We made all the necessary arrangements for his commitment the following day. The last thing he said to me while I was driving him to the airport was, "I'm tired of being unhappy. I don't know how or why but for the first time I feel things are going to change for the better".

Slightly over a year later James called me on the telephone. "I'm ok, I stopped drinking and I'm a believer. I never believed in psychotherapy but now I do. I went through the whole works including group therapy".

I asked him about his future plans and he told me he was going to stay in Athens and start a new practice there. He felt no one here would have confidence in him, they would only remember him as a "drunk".

Moral

Alcohol is the deadliest of drugs. Practically all deaths in traffic accidents are caused by drivers who are intoxicated. It is also responsible for the psychological, somatic and economic destruction of families and individuals. It is among the most difficult of psychological problems to treat but under the right conditions individuals can stop drinking and turn into positive and constructive human beings. To succeed in psychotherapy you must genuinely put your heart and soul into it. The intensity with which a person rejects or denies the need for help is the prime indicator of the severity of the problem. Sometimes we have to place the individual in a situation where he can be assisted to discover this by himself.

AN ANGEL AMIDST

Sofia's husband, Elias, who had heard of my work through others, tried to call me but my telephone number was always unlisted. Desperate, with untiring effort, he found out where I lived and came knocking on my door at six in the morning. He was a baker and had just finished his all night shift. He explained, "My wife's behavior is not of this world. I took her to see a psychiatrist in Athens. He diagnosed her as suffering from an atypical psychosis and suggested medication. Sofia refused to take any. Last week she was driving on the wrong side of the highway and crashed head on with an oncoming car. Fortunately, no one was seriously injured as she was moving very slowly and he had jammed on his brakes before the impact. Would you please come and see her?" I replied, "I'm not sure if I can do anything in this situation but I will visit and see if I can help in any way."

Whether or not I believed that angels walk upon this planet of ubiquitous madness, I met one. She walked across the room with angelic grace, smiled at me and said, "I have been waiting so long for you God, you and I together are going to save this world." Maybe it was my imagination but there seemed to be a glowing white light surrounding her. I looked for a halo and wings but saw none. "Perhaps they are transparent", I empathically suggested to myself.

Elias rarely smiled, struggled to express himself and did not show his feelings easily. As much as he

17

tried to hide it, he was very angry with his wife's illness and behavior. At times he could not control himself and succumbed to physical abuse. Her response was to accept it with a guilt-ridden silence.

Sofia was a nature lover. She had an exquisite sensitivity to all the magnificent displays of nature's grandeur. Every sunset was an ever changing miracle for her. When walking through the country side she would dance with the harmonious movements of the wild flowers. Thus, it was inevitable that our sessions would be spent mostly taking walks along the beach, in full view of the islands sensuous surroundings.

Sofia trusted me so when I explained the importance of her taking medication she offered no opposition.

She was always ready and willing to help others or any worthy cause, so we focused on community projects that would stabilize her behavior. She became a member of the school board which offered many such opportunities, planning school parties and charitable events. Her medication as well as her active participation in down to earth helpful activities kept her thought processes within the bounds of reality. She felt better about herself and benefited from the instant reward of her kindness. She said to me one day, "Even though I know I am not really one, I know what it must feel like to be an angel."

Elias who was always impatient with Sofia felt he could not waste his life waiting for her to get better and decided to divorce her. It did not create any irresolvable hardships for either of them. It had been an arranged marriage that was devoid of love from the start.

We walked and talked and talked and walked on the seemingly endless soft sandy beaches. Her ego was delicately fragile so I made every effort to keep our conversations well grounded in reality.

As often happens, the patient is more intelligent or better informed in some areas than the therapist. Sofia was not a religious person in the usual sense, never went to church but had a profound knowledge of Christian history, the Bible and especially the "Devil's Bible", which contained both the New and Old testaments. She could quote chapter and verse at will. She was uncanny with the details she would at times express. "Jesus was not the son of God but was sent forth by Allah to trick us." "The Devil's Bible", she said on another occasion, "contained three hundred parchment pages made from the skin of donkeys and weighed about a hundred sixty five pounds. On page two hundred and ninety", she said laughingly, "is a funny drawing of the Devil in diapers. Unlike the New and Old Testament which were written in Greek and Hebrew the Devil's Bible was written entirely in Latin by a monk who was supposed to be guided by the Devil but now we know that's not true."

Once, in one of our walks, she stopped, looked around and said, "This area is very familiar to me. It's just like I dreamed where Satan tried to seduce Jesus. I was there watching. When Jesus rejected him I saw Satan turn into a snake and slither away." Sofia had a formidable familiarity with the history of the catholic

Popes even though she had been baptized Greek Orthodox. Whenever Sofia related these historic tales it was never out of need for condemnation or judgment but rather from the saddened realization of the hypocrisy projected upon the world by those who should command the highest respect. Her gracious winning smile was always present no matter who or what she was speaking of. She consistently expressed a humane understanding of the paradoxical nature of man and the tendency of the most wicked to seek and rise to positions of power. Through their influence they created laws which projected the evil within themselves and used them to abuse others. She quoted the Liber Gomorrhianus which was a Papal Treatise issued by the Pope on Papal corruption and sex that had been used to accuse Benedict IX of homosexuality and bestiality. "This", she added "shows how little has changed or been understood by the Catholic church which even today tries to hide the enormous pederasty problems they have with their priests."

"How innocent was innocent IV when he introduced the use of torture to force confessions of heresy during the inquisition. "It's my birthday today". She suddenly burst out laughing, "it reminds me of Pope Alexander VI. If I were a man he would probably bring me a huge cake from which little nude boys would jump out. He was famous for giving huge parties which were similar to orgies. I guess that's where the modern practice of having nude women do the same at stag parties must have started from".

In one our walks, I asked Sofia, "Where did this

profound interest in Christianity come from?" "From as early as I can remember", she answered, "my mother was always critical of the actions of others. She saw nothing but evil, hypocrisy, destruction and inhumanity. At some point, I don't remember when, it all became clear to me. Instead of unifying mankind it has become its greatest divider. In his efforts to control what he does not understand about himself, among other things, he created the "monster" of religion. As always no matter what weapons you devise, be they religion, philosophy or any other kind of theory, it always comes down to the man behind the gun, who you are, in the end, no matter what you believe. Man needs to search within not to create myths to explain his behavior. This always leads to self deception, it's the sad story of mankind".

Unfortunately, we had to terminate our contact as Sofia moved to a home in Athens she had inherited from her parents. I'm not sure who learned more, she from me or me from her. What I do know is wherever she is that place will have the presence of an angel and will be a better place for it.

Moral

To classify, make judgments or generalizations about others without knowing them is simply demonstrating your own insensitivity and ignorance. You may find when you get to know them they are far more of a human being than you are.

THE BABE

Teenagers are natural social communicators. By grouping they create a unique support system to offset the growing pains of adolescence. But that is not true of everyone. Some of us are loners and find it hard to fit in with the rest of the crowd. Babe was such a person.

Our group reveled in athletics, baseball, football, basketball, you name it we played it, that was our world. Babe lived in our neighborhood but had little of that kind of athletic talent. His priorities were different. He started smoking at ten, rarely socialized with anyone and preferred to spend his time in the local billiard parlor. There he excelled and became an outstanding pool player. If his life circumstances had been different he easily could have become a recognized champion. It was amazing to see what he could do with a cue ball.

We grew up during the depression years. The streets of New York were our playing fields. There were fewer cars then so if one parked in our playing area, we just asked them to move farther down the block. Our favorite meeting place was in front of one of the apartment buildings where we sat around on the sidewalk.

During the summer we would open a fire hydrant. One of us would hold a small board up against where the water gushed out, creating a huge spray. It was great fun, gave us something to do and refreshingly saved us from those hot, humid concrete city days. We seldom were able to visit the Long Island beaches or Coney Island. When that rare opportunity arose, we experienced it more like the impossible dream. Eating those delicious Nathan's hot dogs and drinking that free root beer was living in paradise. Kids are magically insensitive to poverty and superbly capable of finding ways to enjoy themselves despite the hardships.

Always searching for, we knew where to find each other, our favorite sitting place. We talked about anything and everything. We can all recall the deeply probing questions that arise in early adolescence. We searched for answers about life and death, God and the universe.

I was the captain of the team. The others referred to me as the "professor" because I loved "philosophizing". They looked up to me and were always asking questions as if I knew the answers. It was a great learning experience for everyone especially for me.

Once, Babe came by, I asked him to join us and he did. Later his visits became more frequent. He always listened but rarely spoke except for an occasional question. I eventually asked him to join our team. We all could see how difficult it was for him but in time he shyly complied. It was hard for some of the team to accept him since they knew it would weaken our chances of winning. I played him in most of our games and it really did not make that much of a difference. In our sidewalk talks we realized we were having fun just being together and rarely if ever, taking things seriously. We learned how to laugh and joke about the "need to win". Only much later did we realize what a significant impact that had on our lives.

As we grew we went off on our different, desired directions. It was close to the end of World War two. I volunteered and joined The U.S. Marine Corps. Within five months the war officially ended and I was assigned to the U. S. Naval Receiving Station in Brooklyn, New York as a prison guard. My regular assignment was to guard the more serious offenders awaiting court martial. One other occasional duty was to transport prisoners from Brooklyn to the Naval Prison in Norfolk Virginia.

During one of those journeys, while walking through the Norfolk compound, I circumstantially met the Babe. He was an inmate. I asked him why he was there. He informed me that he was being court martialed for some serious drug offense.

I did not see or hear from him for many years, until one day there was a knocking at my door. Opening the door, to my great but pleasant surprise, there was the Babe. In his arms he was holding a bouquet of flowers, a box of chocolates and cigars. I invited him in expressing joyfully how happy I was to see him and asked, " what happened?" He had been court martialed and dishonorably discharged. The military tribunal had ordered a psychiatric examination before sentencing. He was diagnosed as schizophrenic and was sent to a psychiatric prison hospital. Puzzled, I asked the obvious question, " how did you get here now?"

A big smile came over his face and he happily asked, "how did you know what to say to me?" I replied, " I don't know what you mean." He went on, "Last week as I was lying on my prison bed, you came to me. Not as you are now but as the "philosopher" we knew as teenagers. I remembered the things we spoke about. I can't explain what happened next. I had what felt like an orgasm and my schizophrenia disappeared. The doctors couldn't believe it. They examined and tested me over and over again until I was finally declared sane and discharged. So here I am. Thanks, "Squanto Gittigans". That was his favorite name for me when we were kids.

In my over fifty years, as a practicing psychologist I have never seen, heard or read of something like that happening. Schizophrenia is presently an incurable disease. Spontaneous remissions are known to occur but they do not last. The Babe died at fifty six without ever having to take medication again. It could have been a misdiagnosis. Yet so many kind acts and miraculous happenings take place every day on this earth, of which we are unaware. Most are never recorded.

I recalled, at that moment, the words of the ancient Greek philosopher, Socrates, who said, "they say I am wise but that's because I'm the only one wise enough to know that I know nothing".

Moral

Spontaneous acts of kindness will always have a beneficial outcome even though you may not know how or when that will be. We all learn from one another but cannot foresee when those learnings become insights or what impact they will have upon our lives. Kindness it seems, not experience, is our best teacher.

THE SEXUALLY SEDUCTIVE MOTHER

To be granted the opportunity to work with a multi-talented individual, for a psychotherapist, is equivalent to finding a buried treasure chest full of gold and diamonds. Frank was just such a person. He was only sixteen, already an excellent swimmer, an outstanding pianist and endowed with a very superior intellect. In high school he was frustrated, subject to frequent temper tantrums and struggling with his studies. His main problem, as he expressed it, "I can't find a girlfriend they all keep rejecting me".

His father was serving a prison sentence for secretly planting and growing Marijuana plants on a small plot of land he owned. Frank was deeply ashamed of and had little if any respect for him. His mother who had taken over the responsibility of raising their three children accepted any work she could find. Mostly this was as a cleaning maid in hotels.

The relationship between his mother and father was at best rocky. She was energetic and dynamic he was fundamentally passive. Frustrated by an apparently sexually unfulfilling husband she turned towards her son to fill the void. It was difficult to evaluate specifically how much sexual interaction had taken place between Frank and his mother. His memories were screened, mostly repressed and vague. There was the suggestion that she had masturbated him as a child. "Once", he told me, "I remember being in bed with my mother, she thought I was asleep and grabbed my

penis. Frightened, I rolled over pretending I was unaware of what was happening."

One of the first things Frank shared with me was a
collection of photographs of his mother posing in the
nude in provocative positions. Throughout his adolescence she walked around the house in the nude or
"sexy" underwear. He blushingly revealed, "it was as
if she kept me in a constant state of tease".

My favorite hobby is underwater archeology. To
be able to join and participate in exploratory expedi-
tions searching for archeological treasures I had to become a master diver. This meant I could train and cer-
tify anyone interested in becoming a scuba diver.
Frank was delighted when I offered to teach him. In
just one year he easily surpassed all of my diving
skills. So much so that ship owners who docked in our
island harbor sought him out to do underwater repairs.
Disgruntled and disappointed with his poor high
school performance, Frank decided to take a course in
computers. Once again, he excelled and found immediate employment as a computer repairman. Continu-
ing with his bent towards the physical, he began to
study the martial arts. Within a short period of time,
using his natural talents, he rose to the level of a cer-
tified teacher. He opened his own school and it was
not long before he had more students than he could
accept. He was a wonderful teacher and his students
worshipped him.

His self-confidence was understandably growing.
Along with his achievements we were working on his
problem with women. In his fourth year of therapy he

entered into a relationship with a woman he eventually married. It was premature, he was not yet ready. It ended in divorce shortly afterwards.

Familiar with Frank's progress and abilities, a friend who was the principal of the local technical high school, offered him a teaching position. There he taught students who like him showed very little interest in academics. Through his personal experiences, Frank was acutely aware of how important it is to challenge the mind of an intelligent child. A child who is easily bored when unchallenged and gives the external impression of being "lazy" or "stupid". He knew intuitively how to do this, mentally and physically with outstanding success.

A handsome lad with a superbly conditioned athletic body, it was inevitable with his mounting achievements and their effect on his self-image that his attitude and approach to women would change. Where before his shyness never allowed him to notice, he was becoming increasingly aware of how many women were attracted to him. He went through numerous flirtations until he met Georgia. They fell deeply in love and decided to marry. A beautiful daughter was born the following year.

Frank was a well spring of talentual surprises. With two other excellent musicians, a trio was formed. Frank began to play the guitar and sing as well. The band was an instantaneous success. Their popularity demanded frequent late night appearances. A potentially dangerous entrapment for Frank. He had grown from a shy, frustrated adolescent, to a confident, gifted performer. Unable to relate to women at the start they were now "falling all over him". The sweet taste of sexual success was too provocative, too stimulating, too much of a temptation to resist. He came to me one day distressed but determined and said, "I'm going to leave my wife. I've been having an affair with a French tourist all summer. She's returning to France and has asked me to go live with her there. He was convinced they were both "really" in love with each other and saw no other solution. I suggested before he made any impulsive move he allow us some time to look into the situation more deeply.

Frank was a truly feeling, sensitive person. Sex can become as it often is, an irresistible, powerful drive in all of us. In those moments, we are all vulnerable to the instantaneous excitement and momentary pleasure it easily affords. We confuse sex with love as if it were one and the same. When the satisfaction of sex takes priority in our lives we become self-deceptive. Fulfillment of our desires takes precedence over our feelings and clouds our judgment. This is exactly what was happening to Frank. In his effort to appease his conscience, he was deluding himself that he was "really in love".

We met to review the issue many times. When he was ready we asked his wife to join the discussions. Frank confessed to her about his affairs. Georgia, needless to say, was shocked. She was totally unaware of what had been going on. It hurt her deeply and it took some time for her to recover but she eventually forgave him. Frank was instantly relieved. He was able to take a giant step in his maturity. He realized what a remarkable person his wife Georgia really was and how much they both loved each other and their family.

Frank became a devoted father and husband. To this day, they have remained a loving, devoted family. In our last conversation, Frank said to me, "I was thinking about the role of sex in our lives. God must have been saddened by those of us who never learned how to love and created sex as a pitiful compromise".

Moral

Sex with the one you love becomes an unsurpassable joy. It blends into but is not the foundation of your happiness. Love's goal is to make those you love feel good about everything which goes far beyond sex.

LIFE IS A BITCH

I had heard of the expression, "if you give a man enough rope he will hang himself" but I never dreamed I would see its actual expression in reality. Jack was a rope salesman. He knew exactly what type and length of rope he needed. He sat for hours under a tree in his backyard fixing a hangman's knot over and over again, contemplating his own death. In one final desperate move, he stood up and tossed the rope over a branch. He tied one end of the rope around the tree trunk, stood on a stool, and tightened the knot around his neck.

He could not tell me later how long he was standing there. All he remembered was at some point, he realized he could not go through with it, loosened the knot and sat on the ground crying. It was the whaling cry of a deeply hurt and tortured soul trapped in the bottomless abyss of a pain without end.

The day before, Jack, not feeling well, decided to close his shop and go home, something very unusual for him as he was compulsively committed to a job that demanded a long day.

He was out of the house by seven AM every day except Sundays and was never home before eight in the evening. It was about noon when he walked into his bedroom and found his wife in bed with his brother.

The shock was so physically intense for everyone that no one said a word. Jack simply turned around,

walked out and roamed the streets for hours in a trau-
matic, amnesic coma. His unconscious automatically
came to his aid. He was repeatedly trying to block out
the scene as if it had never happened.

His brother, Bob, who was married but unem-
ployed was a frequent visitor to his home. He would
often play with the kids. He was particularly warm and
attentive to their mother but Jack always saw that as
brotherly love.

Some months before, Bob's wife Martha had made
an appointment to see me. Bob insisted he come along
even though she did not want him to. He was clearly
suspicious of her motive. What became transparent
during the session was he needed to be sure I was not
her boyfriend. He had not even the slightest desire to
participate. She described him as a loner, unfeeling
and suspicious of everyone's motives no matter who
they were.

Martha eventually moved to Athens. She called to
let me know how she was progressing. "I just want
you to know I'm in a new relationship and pregnant.
It happened very naturally, I didn't even have to think
about it. I'm sorry I couldn't see who Bob was from
the beginning but I'm over the anger now. He helped
me understand what love is not." Originally in their
failed efforts to have a child, Bob blamed Martha.

There are homes in which no child should ever be
condemned to grow up in. Bob and Jack's father was
viciously cruel and physically abusive. He bore not
even the most distant resemblance of what could be
described as a human being. He literally tortured his

entire family both somatically and psychologically.

Jack said to me once, "when he died I did not attend his funeral. If I had I would have driven a stake through his heart. One night, I was only ten years old, he asked me to load some farm supplies on our donkey who was thinned down to the bone and badly mistreated. The donkey refused to move so he picked up a stick and started to beat me. I don't remember how many times he hit me before I slipped out of his grasp and ran away. Then he took out his rage on the poor helpless donkey who he beat to death with the same stick. Another time he had taken a carving knife from the kitchen and went to cut up his wife. It took four men, neighbors who responded to our screams, to stop and subdue him. It was truly miraculous that anyone survived in our family. In substance no one really did. All ten of the children became psychological casualties. Two of my sisters ended up in mental institutions."

Jack's depression was life long, it was simply exacerbated by the current events. The courage in the human soul is not always visible nor is it always reachable. Jack indicated he had that inner strength when he asked for help. I worked with both him and his wife. They finally decided to start all over. She suggested she take the children with her to Sweden where she was born. Jack was to remain behind, sell the house and business, then join them.

It was a cruel deception. Once in Sweden with the children she filed for divorce and told Jack she never wanted to see him again.

How much cruelty and deception can anyone expect a human being to tolerate? To his credit, after years of work together, Jack managed to stand solidly on his own and smile once more. Once touched and uncovered there is more courage in the human heart than the frailties of our humanity sometimes enable us to understand.

Moral

The choices of our partners can never go beyond our understanding of ourselves.

I'M AFRAID TO BE ALONE

Who isn't? It is implied in the fear of death, still we all do not show it in the same way or understand the reason why. We all fear rejection but the idea of being left alone forever places a close second. Maria had to have a friend accompany her when she first came to see me. Her self-deception was well reasoned. "It's ok for her to be here with me since she knows everything about me anyway. May I call you doctor?" Going along with her game playing I replied, "You may call me anything you like as long as it's flatter-ing". That broke the ice and she accepted the sugges-tion we speak without anyone else present.

Maria could not go anywhere alone. To take even a single step outside her front door was impossible without someone being with her. She was like a child with an imaginary playmate with the difference the playmate was always very real. The consequence? She went through many acquaintances who eventually grew tired of her dependency and would abandon her. It was not by chance she always selected someone who took the initiative, criticized and told her what she should do. Nor was it an accident of fate all of her choices had incredibly similar characteristics as those of her mother.

Fears are best overcome by facing them but every-one needs their own time and preparation. To jump into the fire is only possible when you're ready. The time necessary to get there is relative to the individual.

We do not all have the same strengths and fear is an extremely powerful adversary.

Since Maria was too terrified to come to me we began our sessions by me visiting her. The verbally expressed fear is never the real one. Her facial features were extremely beautiful but her overall attraction was diminished by her excessive body weight. Only thirty-one, she was already divorced and the mother of three children. She had married a man with a serious mental disturbance exacerbated by drug abuse, who kept her in a constant state of fear. Physical abuse could erupt at anytime and was frequent. Aside from the child support she received she did work for a while. She lost her job because she was spending an exorbitant amount of time on the internet with personal issues instead of working on her assignments.

Problems with her children were inevitable. In a private consultation, requested by her oldest daughter, she admitted, "I'm not at all interested in boys, I have a girlfriend who is in love with me". She was only twelve years old. A mirror image of her mother she, too, spent most of her day sitting at the computer establishing contacts with other girls. She was failing all of her subjects in school.

The Internet has become the greatest source for social communication in human history, it surpasses all other forms of consolation for lonely and sexually disabled individuals. It has evolved as a formidable playground for all of the sexual deviations known to man.

Discussions about what she was doing all day long on the computer opened the door for exploration of her agoraphobia. Maria clearly exposed her approach to life was that of a frightened little girl totally lacking in self-confidence and severely sexually repressed. She had discovered the internet was a passive person's sexual paradise. Unable to express her natural feelings and desires as a woman directly in the real world, she could hide behind the distant safety of the computer.

As we progressed, her confidence improved sufficiently enough to make dates with the men she was chatting with on facebook. The contacts were initially disastrous. The men turned out to be abusive and sexually dysfunctional. They demanded freakish and weird practices from her. The rendezvous were much easier to make through the crude use of sexually stimulating language to arouse the lonely unfulfilled desires on both sides. The reality of being face to face was very different.

What became strikingly evident in time, was, her genuine fear was not stepping out into the real world but what might happen if she did. As she expressed it, "I was always afraid I would love being a whore or a prostitute, that I would lose control of my sexual impulses. I couldn't believe the disgusting sexual things I was asked to do by these men yet I did them. It opened my eyes and as strange as it was it helped me grow up".

Once we reached this therapeutic plateau, Maria was able to say, "I realize now I never saw myself as a desirable woman that any man could really love. I lived in a world of solitude and buried anger, filled with sexual fantasies I never dreamed would come to life. Then I made the connection of how angry I had always been with my mother who never allowed me to be myself. I'm not as angry as I was and we get along much better with each other now."

How wonderful! Insights of this kind are the quintessence of psychological growth and progress. We could now search for the thus far hidden creative aspects buried within her.

The decoration of her home already showed Maria had an excellent sense of color use and integration. She shyly brought out drawings she had made in the past and hidden in a closet. She began experimenting with cosmetic jewelry and created very interesting and uniquely colorful designs. She displayed and to this day is successfully selling her creations on the internet. As often happens when passivity is overcome the individual goes to the other extreme and becomes extremely productive. So it continues to be with Maria. So too the magnificent turn around with the use of the internet from a self-destructive device to a creative outlet!

Moral

The tools of life are at everyone's disposal. How you use them is a reflection of who you are.

A DIFFERENT KIND OF EXORCISM

All alcoholics are not alike. Eleni's father was the working type. A butcher by trade, he was a paradoxical admixture of what we often see go together, a lover and killer of animals. He had no problem slaughtering them, something that went along with his insensitivity towards humans, but adored his hunting dog which he nurtured and cared for more than his family.

Eleni's mother, grandparents and all the relatives, for generations were fanatical in their interpretation of Christian doctrine and beliefs. They were particularly austere and severe in their adherence to "Christian sexual behavior", especially to the ideal of no sexual intercourse before marriage.

Eleni was only seventeen but was already in a relationship with Jack who was twenty-three. Although Jack consistently pressured her to have sex with him, Eleni had remained steadfastly true to her family values, her virginity above all. Everything seemed to be going fine until she awoke one morning "possessed". A frantic mass hysteria descended upon everyone.

She began spewing out irreverent curse words and sexual innuendos accompanied by somatic simulations. The family all agreed there was only one way to deal with this and immediately called upon the local priest to perform an exorcism.

Eleni's first words to him when he arrived were, "would you like to fuck me?" The young inexperienced priest, caught by surprise was visibly shaken.

He asked if he could use the phone and immediately called the local bishop for assistance and clarification of the procedure that was to be followed. When the Bishop arrived they initiated the required religious incantations, calling on the devil to withdraw from her body, over and over again without success.

The family was not only frantic but completely devastated. They did not know what else to do until their neighbor, a former client of mine suggested that maybe a psychologist could help. This bordered on heresy for them but in their desperate, distraught state they reluctantly agreed to give it a try.

Eleni did not quite say the same things to me she had first said to the priests. She seemed to sense there was something different in my approach. She never really believed in her family's traditional behavior. Her natural instincts were always at war with them. Her feelings were pushing her one way, her conscience another. She was consistently feeling guilty about her normal thoughts and desires.

I visited Eleni regularly every week for two years. The truth is not an easy thing to see especially if you have been bombarded by authoritatively presented myths all of your life. What eventually surfaced, was, the night before the "possession", Eleni gave into Jack's persistent demand for sex. In an attempted compromise effort with her conscience she convinced herself she was not actually having sexual intercourse by allowing Jack to, "take me from behind". The next morning she awoke "possessed".

Moral

We cannot deny what is natural in us. To do so disrupts our physical and psychological balance and usually results in human tragedy.

THE CHARMER

"My insides are rotting". Those were the first words I heard from John. He was my first assignment as a psychology intern. He had voluntarily entered the hospital certain he was dying of some form of cancer. He had undergone every medical test and examination possible. There was clearly no evidence of any somatic complication or problem. He adamantly and persistently refused to accept the findings.

When I asked him why, he confidently retorted, "Because science has not yet found the proper test to uncover the disease I have".

John was six feet tall with blond curly hair, an athletic build and sparkling eyes of ocean blue. He was strikingly handsome. He easily could have been just from looks alone a Hollywood movie star or model. The young nurses on the ward eagerly awaited his service calls or needs just to glance at him.

Before his breakdown, his acquaintances called him the "Rudolph Valentino" of our era. Very few women could resist him. Aware of his good looks he used them with enchanting grace. He became in his young life (he was twenty-eight years old) the epitome of the charming rogue. There was something about him though that gave me an eerie feeling. My first impression was of a certain strangeness I could not explain. I began to understand much later when he started to open up and was able to tell me more specific details about his life.

What I had intuitively experienced, that feeling of strangeness, that something unusual surfaced when he began to describe his romantic affairs. He was not interested in young women. He pursued aged widows and old maids. What they all had in common was they had to be wealthy. Whenever such a woman came into his sphere of operation he went after her like a hungry cat after a mouse. He cunningly played with her in a similar fashion. He was immediately sensitive to their glances and attraction towards him. That set the stage for their entrapment. He never needed to be aggressive in his approach, he simple turned on his sensuous charms and that was it. Almost immediately they were living together in her house sharing the same bed. He was the greatest of lovers. As men who suffer from secondary impotency, his erection could last for hours. It required very little effort to achieve his goal of having his subject fall madly in love with him.

Once John had succeeded he moved on to stage two. He would come home that day seemingly morose and depressed. With a stunningly brilliant performance worthy of a Hollywood Oscar nomination he would relate how an extraordinary business opportunity had been presented to him but that he didn't have the money required for the investment. You didn't have to be a psychic to anticipate her response. She would say, "Darling is that what you're worried about? Whatever is mine is yours, how much do you need?" By this time he was acutely aware of how much she had in her bank account and would "considerately" ask for one thousand dollars less than the total amount. Once he had the money in hand he would disappear from her life forever.

These love trysts went on for years until very unexpectedly his conscience caught up with him and he began suffering from severe pains.

Delusions of this kind are extremely difficult to overcome. Deep into his therapy he looked up at me and pitifully asked "How can you possibly stand working with me? I'm such a horribly disgusting person. How could you or anybody care about me?" I knew them it was the beginning of his recovery. Unless we can see that a problem exists we cannot do anything about it.

Moral

In the absence of conscience we lose all of our humanity.

LUCIFER YOU ARE A PHONY

I met George in the hospital. He was only eighteen and had failed in his attempt to suicide. His uncle who I had worked with in the past had asked if I could visit George to see if I could help in any way. George's father who didn't know me or trust anyone, insisted he interview me before I made any move. Without any prior arrangement, he came arrogantly knocking at my door armed with a psychiatrist at his side.

The family's erratic history had already been made evident to me through the uncle. It would be a kind description to call the father, Robert, the shadiest of characters. He had made a fortune ruthlessly manipulating and cheating the blacks in Africa. He would, for instance, falsely mark the weights on his scales so that when he sold them rice, sugar or flour, they were always shortchanged. Always ending up with far less than the scales "correctly" displayed. In retaliation they once burned down his house.

One other lucrative procedure he had discovered was to derail freight trains and steal their cargo. This went on for years before he was caught in a carefully planned ambush by the police. He was thrown into prison but through his contacts with devious politicians and secret payments he was released in less than three months. He wisely realized it was time to leave and returned to Greece. With his ever present "shrewd business acumen", he quickly invested in real estate and other businesses and became even wealthier.

Our conversation was more of an inquisition. He demanded evidence of my credentials and experience. A prosecuting district attorney could not have asked "crispier" questions. I listened mostly in silence. There was regrettably not the slightest desire present in his hostile questioning to cooperate or suggest a potentially rewarding approach to his son's problems.

My response was simply that I had not yet seen his son. The decision as to how or if I would treat him was still not made. In very clear and emphatic language I informed him of his son's legal rights among which was the right of choice of who his therapist would be. His angry retort was, "then I'm not paying for it"

It would have been fruitless to explain that it did not matter to me. Once Robert revealed his true feelings, he calmed down. The infamous Scrooge would have parted more compassionately with his money. Crudely insensitive, his entire approach and demeanor had made him transparent. You didn't have to be a psychologist to understand the kind of person he was. He was furiously angry with his son. The absence of any feeling or caring was so obvious but not to him. Once his real goal of nonpayment was established, he walked away from our conference satisfied. He was free of financial responsibility as well as future involvement in any treatment procedure,

Interviews done while someone is heavily medicated are not very productive. I visited him once then waited until he was discharged from the hospital. Our first conversation was simply to introduce ourselves to each other, to determine if he wanted to be helped and whether he was comfortable with me as his potential therapist.

George was a massive collection of internal conflicts. The most primitive of his early memories was of his mother chasing him around the kitchen with a carving knife. His recall of it was so vivid you could relive the traumatizing panic as if it was happening that very moment. His desire to visit and get to know his mother was repeated over and over again. His life-long, unfulfilled need to be loved by his mother was heart rendering. He desperately sought for the reassurance that his mother's love for him did exist.

His mother was born in Sweden. Her marriage to Robert was an impulsive decision mandated by an unexpected pregnancy. She was also an alcoholic something completely unacceptable to Robert who divorced her after the birth of a second child two years later. George never saw his mother again until some years later fortified by the gains he had made in therapy he searched and found her.

It was not just his mother and father who generated the problems in George's life. His grandfather was a uniquely frightening story teller of supernatural myths. He was especially capable with dead spirits and ghosts who he stressed came out at night and were lurking everywhere. His most frightening tales were of the devil who could assume any shape or form and appear before you at any moment. Think about what you are most afraid of, multiply it by a hundred and you may come close to the terror George experienced when he just tried to repeat those stories about the

"Prince of Darkness".

We began taking walks at night along the beach far from town. Whatever light existed was supplied by the brilliance of the stars or the glow of the moon. On one of those nights, I purposely waited for the darkest, we sat down on the sand. Without giving any warning, I yelled as loudly as I could, "OK you so called terrifying Prince of Darkness show yourself, I'm challenging you to a fight". I've seen rockets that couldn't take off as fast as George did that moment It took all my endurance to catch up with him and calm him down. We sat and discussed the incident for a long time afterwards.

George was not so keen on taking those walks with me after that. Somewhere down deep within him though was the realization that something good or positive had happened. This is what every therapist, I believe, looks for in everyone they are trying to help. Most people are more courageous than they believe. George began to show that when as terrified as he was he did not quit on me. To be afraid is human. Time and patience are critical essentials in our search for understanding.

As we moved forward George showed it was within him in different ways. He identified with the weak, poor and disabled, especially older persons who were unable to help themselves. He did everything in his power to assist them. Once he put himself in jeopardy with the police. He had witnessed dome crooked police making a deal with some drug dealers and revealed it publicly. His father sided with the police. He offered the excuse that his son had tried to commit suicide was not well and anything he said was the result of his mental disturbance. It was a graciously accepted explanation for the entire matter which allowed the crooked policemen to escape conviction. No one paid attention to him afterwards but inside himself George knew what the truth was.

We took many, many walks in the night, each time calling out the devil. We called him the worst of cowards until we ran out of epithets. The terror lessened and the fear gradually disappeared. What George began to realize was despite all the threats and denigrating words thrown at him, the devil never showed up. We bolstered this later by sitting in a cemetery and making jokes about our surrounding neighbors who never broke their silence or joined our conversations.

I must admit it was very reassuring for both of us. I truly do not know or can imagine what we would have done if someone actually showed up and started talking to us.

Moral

Children are like sponges with superb powers of absorption. We must be critically aware of what we teach, say or do in front of them. We are responsible for the consequences.

YOU NEVER KNOW

One of the most gratifying fascinations of dynamic psychotherapy is you can never predict its outcome. It begins as a somewhat indecipherable mystery. There is a gradual collection of clues, slowly building into insights, often leading to dramatic changes, sometimes a surprise ending.

Maria was referred by a colleague. To make her appointment, she had to drive three hours from her upstate New York residence, something she did consistently for nine years without once missing an appointment or ever coming late. A small miracle in itself considering the inclement weather and difficult driving conditions she at times encountered.

If she had tripped upon entering she could have rolled over to where I was sitting, such were her bodily contours, almost the duplicate of a large wine barrel. Her dress was accommodatingly designed to cover up what she was clearly embarrassed by. Maria was accompanied by her sixteen-year-old son, Giuseppe. The family had only arrived from Italy about three years earlier.

Speaking with a heavily accented, broken English, she explained her son had a serious problem. All of his teachers had told her that he would never make it academically. He was failing all of his subjects and they insisted it would be best if she withdrew him from school and found some work he could do. This was not the worst of it. Lately he was walking in his sleep. While awake, he was always "a quiet, good boy". During his sleep walking he was throwing things around, banging on doors, turning over furniture and yelling obscenities in very clear English.

I informed Maria if we were to be successful in resolving Giuseppe's difficulties, I would have to work with her as well. At first she resisted, claiming she did not speak English very well and that we would be unable to communicate or understand one another. Only after considerable discussion did she reluctantly agree to try. We arranged to have two consecutive sessions every time we met, one for her and one for her son. This was the first step in what was to become an unpredictable nine-year journey.

While it appeared her son had the more urgent problem the opposite turned out to be true. Somnambulism is basically the response to the frustrations we are unable to overcome in our waking state. Most of us do it through dreaming. The sleepwalker is apparently more blocked and unable to make use of the defense mechanisms available to most of us.

What appeared to be a surface wasteland turned out to be a deceptive veneer concealing a reserve of untapped treasures resting below. With the invaluable assistance of time his keen intellect and inner strengths emerged. He went on to graduate high school and college. He received an MA in Education and became a guidance counselor and football couch in a local high school.

Maria was a different, more intriguing story. Unsurprisingly Giuseppe's growth bore a consistent synchronicity with hers.

Her first words to me were, "I never sleep". "What do you do all night long?" I asked. "I walk back and forth checking if the doors and windows are locked or the gas stove is turned off. I do that all-night long. Sometimes I look out of the windows to see if anything or anybody is outside. I keep this up until everybody wakes up." "How long has this been going on?" "Since we came to America". "Have you been examined by any doctor?" "I went to a neurologist who said I had a problem with my pituitary gland and I take medicine which he prescribed everyday for it".

Her broken English was amazingly not so broken as our sessions continued. I asked if she felt the medication was helping her. She answered, "I don't know. What I remember is before I began taking it, I did sleep one or two hours in the early morning." I muttered to myself, "This needs a closer look, we'll see". Four months into the therapy I suggested, "Maria, I would like to try an experiment with you if you are willing". "Only if it doesn't hurt or make me fatter" she replied with a smile.

This was the first revelation of the many unforeseeable inner strengths she possessed, a delightful sense of humor. The morose, depressed Maria of the past from then on no longer made an appearance. This was accompanied by a remarkable clarity in her expression of the English language. Our explorations into her inner self became creative fun.

We began searching for other well concealed evidence of the true Maria. "I love to bake cakes and pastries", she said one day. "Every time I bake something for my family or friends they tell me how delicious it is". "Did you ever consider doing it for a living?", I asked. "No, but lately a lot of people are suggesting that I should". "Why don't you give it a try?", I offered.

In our next meeting, Maria reported she had discussed the possibility of opening her own bakery, with her husband and he was very supportive. He operated a very successful landscaping business so money was not an issue.

Her business acumen was uncanny, within a month she had found a place, equipped it and was ready to open. People drove from long distances to find her once her reputation spread. Her products were not only incredibly delicious but masterpieces of artistic creativity. In less than a year she was so successful that by noon each day she had nothing else to sell. This culminated in whatever she sold had to be ordered in advance.

Her growing self-confidence steadily improving, her concentration turned towards her appearance and femininity. With the grim determination, she had shown throughout and her irrepressible humor, she winked at me and said, "This fat lady ain't gonna be no more". "Yesterday, I did something I've always wanted to do but was always embarrassed by what I looked like. I signed up to take tennis lessons". What followed only proved that truth can not only at times be stranger than fiction but truly much more magnificent.

In just one year that wine barrel shaped woman who first walked into my office, had transformed into a thirty-six inch bust, twenty six- inch waist, thirty-six inch hips figure who could challenge the most beautiful of models. The icing on this human cake, she had so long labored to create came in our next to last session. "Last night", she proudly announced with a pixyish smile and slight roll of her hips, "I beat my tennis instructor in three straight sets". We both almost choked with empathic laughter.

Moral

Never take anything for granted or judge by appearances. The quintessential human quality which guides wisdom to understanding is feeling.

Other books by the author:

A Poetry of Human Feelings

The Life of Sosat Silacay

When a child goes silent

www.ingramcontent.com/pod-product-compliance
Lightning Source LLC
Chambersburg PA
CBHW060221290526
45789CB00003B/1360